The Corduroy Road

The Corduroy Road

PATRICIA EDWARDS CLYNE

Illustrated by Cary

DODD, MEAD & COMPANY
New York

Text copyright © 1973 by Patricia Edwards Clyne
Illustrations copyright © 1973 by Cary
All rights reserved
No part of this book may be reproduced in any form
without permission in writing from the publisher
ISBN: 0-396-06815-4
Library of Congress Catalog Card Number: 73-3902
Printed in the United States of America

To
my family,
who patiently endure
my "Revolutionary Rambles"

Author's Note

STRANGELY ENOUGH, it was a new highway that led to the discovery of an ancient one. For in 1954, during the construction of the New York State Thruway, the Corduroy Road was uncovered at the bottom of a lake at the northern end of Tuxedo, New York.

Built in 1778, from a map drawn by Robert Erskine, Military Engineer for General George Washington, the road was only four-and-a-half miles long. However, during the Revolutionary War it served as part of a vital alternate communications and supply route between Morristown, New Jersey, and West Point, New York. (The regular route, the Orange Turnpike, was closer to the Hudson River, and could be cut off by the British.)

Some of the corduroy sections—massive, hand-hewn logs—are now on display at Washington's Headquarters Museum, Newburgh, New York.

Contents

The Corduroy Road

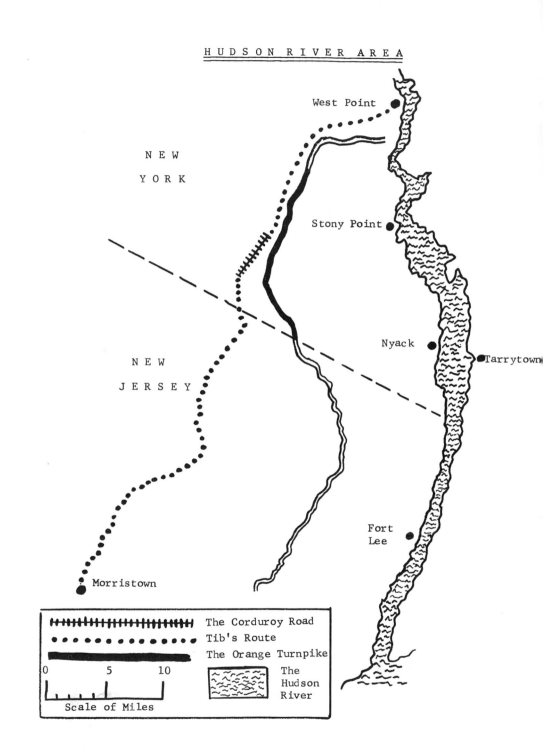

HUDSON RIVER AREA

West Point

NEW
YORK

Stony Point

NEW
JERSEY

Nyack

Tarrytown

Fort
Lee

Morristown

The Corduroy Road
Tib's Route
The Orange Turnpike

The
Hudson
River

0   5   10

Scale of Miles

1

The Sound in the Loft

WHEN HE ENTERED THE BARN, Tib thought he heard something move up in the hayloft, but he couldn't be sure. Probably just a mouse, he decided, as he waited for his eyes to adjust to the dim light.

What a relief to be out of the hot July sun. At least he wouldn't have to go out in the fields today—not since that British Major had brought in his horse for Tib's uncle to treat.

Tib frowned as he bent over to pick up the pail of water. Imagine Uncle Edward treating British horses and supplying the Redcoats with food. A Tory! A man who sympathized with the British while his fellow Americans were fighting— and dying—for their independence!

The thought of death made tears sting Tib's eyes. His own father had died only three months ago, after an accident at the furnace.

Tiberius Wade, Sr. had lived only long enough to tell his son, "Go to your Uncle Edward. He will take you to live with him—maybe even teach you to be a horse doctor and a farmer. But if for some reason Edward can't take you, then go to my sister Jenny in Morristown. Go by way of the Corduroy Road. It's safe. Remember, the Corduroy Road is . . ."

Tib had bent down to catch the rest of what his father said. But there were no more words. Tiberius Wade, Sr. was dead.

Sadly packing his clothes and the tools his father had owned, Tib had walked the few miles to Stony Point, New York, where Uncle Edward lived.

Uncle Edward had welcomed him at first. But as the days passed, Tib felt his uncle was displeased with him for some reason. Tib did not know why. Surely, he worked long and hard to help his uncle.

Could it have anything to do with the questions Uncle Edward was always asking? Tib would have gladly answered anything except questions about the iron furnace where his father had worked. For Tiberius Wade, Sr. had often warned his son, "Do not tell anyone what you know about the work going on at the furnace. You never know who may be a British spy."

Tib had done as his father told him. Every time Uncle Edward asked about the furnace, Tib would deny any knowledge of what was being made there.

Exasperated at last, his uncle had roared, "You're lying, Tib! You know what's going on down there. Tell me. Are they forging another huge chain to span the Hudson? The fools! Do they think that will stop the British from capturing West Point?"

Tib had only stared at his uncle, suspicion forming in his mind. Was his uncle a Tory—a friend of the British?

His question was answered a few days later when the British captured the nearby fort at Stony Point. Uncle Edward did not attempt to hide his delight as the red-coated soldiers swarmed through the town.

It was on that day, May 30, 1779, that Tib knew he must run away from Uncle Edward.

But just as if he had read the boy's mind, Uncle Edward had taunted Tib, "And don't try running away, Tib. I need your help here. If you run away, I'll have the soldiers after you. And when they catch you, I may not take you back. I may have them take you to serve as a cabin boy on one of their ships. And you know what kind of a horrid life that would be!"

Tib had shivered and the man laughed. "Imagine what your father would say if he knew his son was aiding the British! He never even knew *I* was working for them!"

"A spy!" Tib had blurted out.

Uncle Edward had smiled coldly. "A friend, Tib. A friend

who keeps his eyes and ears open—and also doctors their horses."

Just then the horse whinnied weakly. Tib jumped in surprise. He had been so busy thinking he had almost forgotten why he was in the barn. The horse whinnied again from the stall. British or not, the horse was sick and probably thirsty. So once more Tib picked up the heavy wooden pail and held it as the animal drank.

While waiting for the horse to finish, Tib's eyes focused on a shaft of sunlight. Idly, he followed the dust-speckled beam from the floor of the barn up to the hayloft where it entered through a crack between the roof boards.

Suddenly Tib stiffened.

The sunbeam had struck something that glistened—glistened like steel.

Just the pitchfork, Tib reasoned, and returned his attention to the horse. That is, until he remembered the pitchfork in the loft was made of wood—all wood. And wood did not glisten in the sun!

2

A Dangerous Discovery

CURIOSITY OVERCAME his reluctance to climb up the ladder to the hot dusty loft. Shoving aside the balky trapdoor, Tib's head was soon level with the loft floor. At first he could see nothing, for the shaft of sun blinded him. Moving his head to the side, out of the sunbeam, he found himself staring into a pair of bloodshot blue eyes!

The shock made Tib lurch back and he would have fallen off the ladder, had not a hand reached out to clutch his shoulder.

Tib began struggling—fighting to free himself—to get down the ladder to safety.

"Calm yourself, boy," came a panting whisper, "or you'll get this knife between your ribs!"

Terror made Tib freeze to the ladder rungs.

"Now, up with you, lad," came the voice again. "I have no desire to hurt you."

The pressure of the hand on his shoulder increased, and Tib forced himself up, knees trembling, onto the floor of the loft.

"What's your name, lad?"

When Tib told him, the black-haired man let out a short laugh. "Tib, is it? What kind of name is that?"

Anger burned away his fear and Tib shot back, "It's short for Tiberius—Tiberius Wade, Jr."

A smile played at the corners of the man's pale lips, then disappeared as he frowned. "Is this your father's farm? How far are we from . . ."

Just then the man began to sway unsteadily. Gesturing for Tib to do the same, he sat down—in fact, almost fell—in the pile of hay.

Tib stared at the dirt-streaked stranger, noticing the glassy eyes and the shallow breathing. Though the loft was fiercely hot under the July sun, there was not a droplet of perspiration anywhere on the man's face. He's sick, Tib realized. He's terribly sick!

"Well, lad, I asked you a question."

The voice was weak but determined, and the hand still held the knife only inches from Tib's chest.

"It's my Uncle Edward's farm," Tib explained. "He's . . . he's a horse doctor."

"How far from the fort at Stony Point?"

"Just west of it," Tib answered.

With a heavy sigh, the man murmured, "Then I'd not come as far as I thought." His head fell forward as if in utter despair.

For the first time Tib noticed his attire. Though torn and caked with mud, the coat seemed to be part of a uniform.

It was not British! was Tib's first thought. And there was something different about the man's speech. It might have been due to the stranger's illness, but Tib was certain he could not be a New York man.

"Who . . . where did you . . ." Tib began.

The man's head shot up. "Tory or patriot?" he demanded.

The choice of words told Tib which side the man was on, and he answered with shame, "My Uncle Edward is a Tory."

"And you, lad?"

"American!" Tib answered proudly.

The man's eyes studied him carefully. "American because you know I am, or American because you believe in independence?"

Anger once more surged through Tib. "My father helped forge the chain that stretches across the Hudson, protecting West Point!"

"If that's so, then you won't mind getting me some water," the man remarked. "Go fetch some, young Tib. I'm much in need of it."

Tib scurried for the ladder, saying, "I've got to go to the well just outside the barn."

The man nodded, his hand reaching under the hay. "Just remember there's a window up here—Long John and I will be watching."

Tib felt a chill shudder through him as a long musket was pulled from the hay.

So the stranger did not believe him, after all!

A dozen questions hurtled through his mind as Tib took the pail to the well. But they were questions which only the stranger could answer, and so Tib hurried back into the barn.

After drinking his fill and splashing his grayish face with some of the water, the man looked up at Tib, then patted the musket at his side. "Long John always insures prompt and confidential service," he said.

Tib snorted. "Your musket had nothing to do with it. I did it because I wanted to—because I'm an American too. I knew you wouldn't dare shoot off your musket with the Redcoats all around!"

The man's eyes narrowed as he gazed at Tib. Then a smile curved his lips. "You're a bright lad, Tib. I'm glad you're on . . . on our . . . side. . . ."

Tib caught the swaying figure before he fell, easing the man's now trembling body to the floor of the loft.

"What's wrong?" Tib asked. "Are you injured?"

"Fever," the weak voice replied. "Must have caught it the night before last . . . spent it in the swamp at the foot of the fort. . . ."

"Then you're . . ." Tib began.

"Lieutenant Jason Harnett of the North Carolina Brigade."

North Carolina! So that was the answer to why this man's speech sounded so strange. But what was a North Carolina soldier doing at Stony Point, New York?

"We're here to recapture the fort," Harnett explained, before Tib could ask. "We're a motley force, to say the least. Besides my North Carolina men, the Light Infantry is made up of soldiers from Connecticut, Pennsylvania, Maryland, Massachusetts, and Virginia. But we'll do the job. The Redcoats will not hold Stony Point much longer!"

Then Harnett went on to relate how he and two other men had been sent, under cover of darkness, to observe the British garrison at Stony Point. They were to report back to their commanding officer, General Anthony Wayne. The other two had gone ahead. Harnett had stayed behind to gather any last-minute information. Then just as he had started back, the fever had struck, causing him to hide in the barn, unable to travel.

"If there is a message you want delivered . . ." Tib began.

"No, Tib, though you're a brave lad to offer. The important thing is that I'm not caught by the Redcoats. If they find me, they'll know something is afoot. Our only chance is a surprise attack on the fort."

"You'll not be caught!" Tib declared.

A sudden tremor shook Harnett's whole body, but he managed to say, "Thank you, Tib. I was not mistaken when I decided to trust you. You are an American, indeed!"

Pride made Tib straighten his shoulders, and he was about to say something more, when a new sound—only barely heard —made him listen intently.

"It's my uncle," Tib whispered. "He must be looking for me. I'll be back as soon as I can."

3

The Linseed Poultice

As HE EMERGED into the sunshine of the bright July afternoon, Tib blinked rapidly. "Coming, Uncle," he called, his sun-blinded eyes barely making out the huge figure of his Uncle Edward standing in the doorway of the house.

"Where have you been, Tib?" his uncle demanded, as they entered the kitchen together.

"The . . . the horse was very thirsty. I stayed to make sure he was no worse."

"Good lad!" came another voice—a strange one.

Tib looked around to see the bright-red uniform of a British major. Without thinking, the boy's eyes sought the window, then gazed at the barn from which he had come—the barn where Jason Harnett lay sick in the loft.

The British major noticed Tib's glance, but mistook its significance. "Yes, it's my horse, lad," he said. "I hope you're keeping a watchful eye."

"Y . . . yes," Tib stammered. "A . . . a watchful eye."

"I'll be out to see him anon," the major went on.

"Oh, no," Tib murmured, then realized he had spoken out loud.

But the major didn't seem to notice what Tib said, for he had turned to Uncle Edward. "Your son?" he asked.

Uncle Edward shook his head. "My nephew—my dead brother's child. Since I am unmarried, Tib is going to be my son now. That is, as soon as he gets over some of his wild ideas."

The son of a Tory? Tib almost shouted. Never! Little did Uncle Edward know that he would not be there much longer. As soon as he could, he was going to run away to Morristown, where Aunt Jenny lived. But Morristown was in New Jersey —more than forty miles from Stony Point. . . .

Tib looked up suddenly when he heard his uncle say his name. "We'll be out to look at the horse as soon as the afternoon cools some. I don't want to lance that boil in such heat."

Tib couldn't help wondering whether Uncle Edward was more concerned about himself or the horse, but he said nothing.

"Keep putting those warm poultices on the boil, Tib, and give the beast plenty of water."

Nodding, Tib stood there until the two men went back into the parlor to wait out the afternoon heat. Then he stirred the fire to warm the linseed meal for the poultice.

As he worked, Tib thought again of what Uncle Edward had said. Would he expect Tib to become a British spy too?

"Never!" Tib repeated, this time out loud.

He knew he must go to Aunt Jenny in Morristown, but how? Forty miles on foot? There was always the threat of marauding Indians, but that was not the worst danger. The British were all around here, and Uncle Edward had said he would send the Redcoats after him if he tried to run away. Even if he could get to the Orange Turnpike, Tib knew it was not safe. Though General Washington used it to convey supplies between Morristown and West Point, it was often cut off by the British.

His father's last words flashed into Tib's mind, as they had done every day since Tib learned that Uncle Edward was a Tory.

Go by way of the Corduroy Road. It's safe. Remember, the Corduroy Road . . .

But Tib had no idea where the Corduroy Road might be and he certainly couldn't ask Uncle Edward about it. It was such an odd name that Tib wondered if maybe his father's mind had been wandering when he said this.

Did he dare ask Jason Harnett? Would the lieutenant laugh at him? Would he tell him if there was such a road? What if it was some secret route? Did the sick soldier trust him enough to tell him even if he did know?

Well, it would do no harm to ask, Tib decided, as he lifted the small pot of steaming linseed meal and left the kitchen.

4

A Dream Destroyed

THE SUN SEEMED EVEN HOTTER when Tib paused at the well to refill the bucket, and he was panting by the time he entered the barn.

Glancing up to the loft, Tib gestured toward the stall of the sick horse. If Jason Harnett was watching, he gave no sign. The poor animal was breathing heavily, its eyes filled with pain. Tib wished he could have some help in applying the poultice, but he knew better than to ask Uncle Edward. More than once in the last three months he'd had the taste of a strap across his bare legs for "being lazy," as his uncle judged it.

The horse tried to kick Tib when the hot poultice touched the agonizing boil, but Tib jumped aside. Once the animal pinned him against the side boards of the stall, then moved away, too wracked with pain to stand still for very long.

Sweat was pouring from his body when Tib finally climbed the ladder to the loft.

"That was a man's job," Jason Harnett commented, obviously having observed Tib's doctoring of the horse.

"But I did it!" Tib retorted.

"I meant no insult, young Tib," the lieutenant apologized. "Just that you could have used some help."

Tib looked away. There was no sense in telling his troubles to Lieutenant Harnett. The man had misfortune enough of his own. So instead, Tib asked, "Are you feeling better?"

"I slept a bit while you were away, but I can't say I'm any better. My head . . . it . . . sometimes my mind seems to wander . . . and I feel I am burning up."

"Indeed, you are," Tib said, touching his hand to the soldier's dry, ashen skin. "I must get you something to break the fever."

"You're a good lad, Tib," the lieutenant murmured, his eyes half closed. Tib thought he was dozing off, but suddenly he asked, "What brought you here to live with a Tory?"

With as few words as possible, Tib explained how he had come to Stony Point. Lieutenant Harnett said nothing, only nodding from time to time, his eyes still half closed. However, when Tib mentioned the Corduroy Road, Harnett sat bolt upright.

"You've heard of it then?" Tib asked excitedly. "Then there really is a Corduroy Road! Oh, please, Lieutenant, tell me how to get to it!"

At first Jason Harnett only sat there studying Tib with his piercing blue eyes. Then he sighed. "Since your father knew of the Corduroy Road, I see no reason you should not know too. But I dislike being the one to disappoint you after you have been so kind to me."

"Disappoint ..." Tib began. "But if there is such a road, then surely I can get to ..."

He stopped when he saw the lieutenant was shaking his head slowly from side to side.

"It's not like a public highway, Tib," he explained. "It's a secret road used strictly as a communications route for the Continental Army. Also to convey supplies between Morristown and West Point. Unless you have a military pass..."

Tib turned his head away so the lieutenant would not see the tears that were flooding his eyes. But Jason Harnett knew.

"I'm sorry, Tib." His voice was soft with sympathy. "You know, it's not even much of a road. Just a narrow track with logs laid side by side—like corduroy."

Tib's shoulders stiffened at the word which had stood for hope and escape from Uncle Edward, but now meant nothing. He barely heard the lieutenant's words as Harnett went on:

"General Washington had it built last year because the regular route—the Orange Turnpike—was closer to the Hudson and could easily be cut by the British, as it is now. In any event, Tib, it does not run all the way to Morristown. It connects with other roads—dangerous roads—too dangerous for a lad alone."

Tib scrambled to his feet. His heart was heavy, but the tears were no longer in his eyes. "Well, there may be no help for me," he said quietly, "but we must help you."

Quickly, he told the lieutenant that Uncle Edward and the major would be coming to the barn as soon as it was cooler.

"I'll try to get back before they do," Tib added. "But if I can't, just lie still until they go. Then I'll bring you some medicine if I can."

Tib did not notice it but the lieutenant's own eyes were filled with tears as the brave boy descended the ladder once more. How he wished he could help Tib get to Morristown. But even if he directed Tib to the Corduroy Road, he had no authority to issue the boy a military pass.

5

Medicine for a Sick Soldier

Tib had been in the kitchen only a few moments when his uncle came in from the parlor. "Well, boy, what's the word on the major's horse?"

"The poor animal is suffering greatly," Tib reported. "The boil is ready for lancing." Then he could not help adding, "In fact, it's been ready for hours now."

Uncle Edward's eyebrows shot up a full inch. "And what would you know about horse-doctoring?" he demanded. "I'll lance it at sundown—not before. You are lucky, Tib, that I am entertaining a guest. Or else you might be given a lesson in how to hold a hasty tongue!" Then brushing past Tib, he picked up a decanter from a shelf and returned to the parlor.

But his uncle's threat had little effect on Tib, who was already searching one of the shelves that lined the wall. He had been only nine years old when his mother had died, but he still remembered the fever that had burned through her body

34

—a fever much like the one Lieutenant Harnett was suffering from now.

What was it the doctor had given her? Tib tried desperately to remember. But there was really no need, for the answer was right on the label in front of him, spelled out in a faded brownish-black ink: "Tincture of Quinine—for fevers—2 drams."

Clutching the small bottle firmly, Tib made his way out to the barn and up to the loft.

"Quinine!" Jason Harnett exclaimed, when Tib showed him the bottle. "I haven't seen any of that for many months. So many of our lads have died of the fever, but there's no quinine to be had. . ." His voice trailed off as he lay back in the hay.

Tib helped him get the medicine to his mouth, then glanced out of the one small window in the loft. The sun was almost to the top of the tall oak. "The afternoon is on the wane," he told the lieutenant. "Remember, when my uncle and the major come to treat the horse, stay as still as you possibly can."

Harnett nodded, but his eyes did not seem to be seeing Tib.

"Are you all right?" the boy asked anxiously.

Again the lieutenant nodded feebly. "Yes. It's just that my head feels . . . strange. But I . . . I'll be all right."

Tib frowned worriedly. The lieutenant's words sounded slurred, as if he was having difficulty remembering how to pronounce them.

"I'll try to get back once more before they come to lance the boil. Just rest now," Tib urged.

But the lieutenant, whose eyes were not closed, did not appear to have heard him.

6

The Fever Rages

AFTER CHECKING ON THE HORSE and bringing the suffering animal more water, Tib walked slowly back to the house. If Uncle Edward intended to lance the boil after sundown, he would need light, and would chide Tib if any of the candles were low inside the lanterns.

Tib wished that Mrs. Ames, Uncle Edward's housekeeper, were here. But she had left a fortnight ago for Tarrytown, to help her daughter, who was expecting a baby. She wouldn't be back for at least a month—and so all the household tasks had fallen on Tib's shoulders, in addition to his regular duties.

Well, Tib thought, I won't be here when Mrs. Ames does come back. I'm leaving—running away—no matter what happens. I only stayed this long, hoping to find out about the Corduroy Road. Well, now I found out, however little good it does me.

Though it was a decision which spelled danger, Tib felt

better for having made it. And with new vigor he set about replacing the candles in the lanterns.

A little later, Tib picked up the two lanterns. They would serve as an excuse to return to the barn. He would have them there, ready to be lighted, when Uncle Edward arrived.

Setting down the lamps in order to unlatch the barn door, Tib was aware of the thrashing sounds coming from inside. The poor horse, Tib thought. It must be suffering terribly.

But it was not the horse!

As soon as he had stepped into the barn, Tib realized the sound was coming from above—from the loft!

Racing up the ladder and sliding open the trapdoor, Tib halted at the top rung, his eyes wide with shock. Not three feet away from him, Lieutenant Harnett was tossing wildly about on the floor, his voice growing louder as he called, "Now, men. Muskets to the fore. Steady now. Hold your fire. Andrew, take careful aim. They'll be here in . . ."

The lieutenant's voice trailed off into unclear mumbling as Tib scrambled over to him.

"Lieutenant Harnett. It's Tib."

"Tib?" the sick man murmured, turning to look at Tib. His blue eyes were blank. "Tib?" he repeated, then his voice rose again. "Well, yes, now shoulder that musket. Man that redoubt. The Redcoats are to be here soon!"

Tib could only stare in fear as the lieutenant raved on, his

voice sometimes loud, then lowering to a senseless babbling.

For long minutes Tib stood there watching the fever-ridden body roll and thrash on the hay-covered floor of the loft. His own mother had suffered like that before she had died, and memories of that horrible night came rushing back to Tib.

Then another thought flashed through his brain. Uncle Edward would be coming to the barn soon. He'd hear the lieutenant! The lieutenant would be caught by the British and the attack on Stony Point would be ruined!

Tib stood there only a moment longer before he rushed down the ladder, pulling the trapdoor closed behind him. At least the lieutenant wouldn't fall through if he chanced to roll near the opening in the loft floor.

7

A Frantic Search

His shadow raced in front of him, long and black, telling Tib that the afternoon was almost gone. Could he find what he needed? And even if he did find it, would he have time?

There were so many bottles on Uncle Edward's drug shelf! How would he ever know which was the right one? All Tib remembered was that the name began with an "L." The doctor had given some to his mother to quiet her terrible restlessness, but what was the name of the drug? "Lid . . . lad . . . lady . . . it sounded something like that."

Tib almost sobbed at his inability to remember, as he searched through the small bottles and boxes that held his uncle's medicines. He was so intent that he did not hear the door open or the sound of heavy boots on the bare wooden floor.

"And what might you be doing, Tib?"

The boy spun around, eyes and mouth wide open in shock.

Uncle Edward stood there, hands clasped behind his back. "I . . . I was looking for . . . for . . ." Tib stammered.

"My set of lancets is not there!" Uncle Edward bellowed. But his voice was less sharp when he added, "But you were right to try and prepare my instruments, Tib. The lancet case is over there on the settle. Mind you, put a sharp edge on them. The major and I will be out within the hour. Now where is that mutton leg? We'll have a bite before we work."

But the "bite" did not include Tib. For without another word, Uncle Edward found the leftover leg of mutton in the cooling box and then walked out of the kitchen to rejoin the British major.

Tib did not even feel hungry. Nor was he hurt by his uncle's neglect. The boy's mind was on only one thing: finding the medicine that would help Lieutenant Harnett.

Bottles! Boxes! Vials!

Fennel! Cassia! Calomel!

So many names—but none of them starting with "L." Then Tib spied a dust-covered bottle at the back of the shelf.

"Laudanum." That was the name! Tib recalled it now, as he read the handwriting on the label which told him the dosage.

Tib hesitated. Laudanum was a powerful drug. Tib remembered his mother had gone right to sleep after being given a dose of it. Did he dare to give this to the lieutenant? What if he gave him the wrong amount? But the dosage was right there on the label. And if he didn't put the lieutenant to sleep, Harnett would surely be discovered when Uncle Edward and the British major went out to the barn. So, there was only one thing to do.

Picking up the bottle and one of his uncle's tiny measuring cups, Tib raced back to the barn.

8

The Operation in the Barn

THE LIEUTENANT WAS NOT THRASHING AROUND when Tib reached the loft, but his blue eyes still held their wild look. As Tib bent over him, the lieutenant twisted suddenly, grabbing the musket, which he held pointed at Tib:

"A deserter!" came his hoarse cry. "You'll not run away from the fight. Try again and I'll . . ."

Tib's breath halted somewhere between his mouth and lungs, and his chest ached. But he held his ground.

"H . . . here . . . take this." He tried to stop his voice from quivering, but he could not. "General Wayne's orders," Tib added, with sudden inspiration.

Half the laudanum spilled on the floor as he gave the medicine cup to the scowling lieutenant.

Again Tib held his breath until the sick man had swallowed it all. Then he waited as the lieutenant's loud words gradually were reduced to rumbling muttering, then low mur-

muring, and finally deep, heavy breathing.

With a silent prayer that the lieutenant would not snore, Tib once more went down the ladder to return to the farmhouse.

But there was no need, for Uncle Edward was already approaching the barn, the British major right behind him on the narrow footpath.

"So there you are, Tib. Out here again. You must have great regard for the major's horse."

"Yes," Tib answered quietly. "I care about him." But his eyes were on the loft as he spoke.

The actual lancing of the boil took only minutes, but for Tib it was as if hours were slowly passing. Dutifully, he handed Uncle Edward the things he called for, but the boy kept glancing upward—to the loft.

"You'd best keep your eyes on what I'm doing," Uncle Edward grunted, as he lanced the angry-looking boil on the horse's shoulder.

"The lad may have a squeamish stomach," said the major, who was standing at his horse's head, trying to soothe the suffering beast.

Uncle Edward paused to look around at Tib and frown. "He'll get over that soon enough if he's going to live with me!"

But I'm not! Tib wanted to shout. I'm going to Morristown. That is, I'm going as soon as I help Lieutenant Harnett.

And once again he looked up at the loft.

Had he heard a sound, a voice—someone restlessly stirring on the hay-covered floor above? No, it could only have been his imagination. For his uncle and the British major obviously had not heard anything, and were now preparing to leave the barn.

When they got to the door, the major hesitated. "Perhaps I had better . . ." he began.

"I'll watch over the horse," Tib offered at once.

"Good lad," the major smiled. "After all, I must be getting back to the fort."

Tib sighed in relief when he heard their footsteps crunch off into the deepening twilight. He was hungry now, terribly hungry, for he had not eaten since breakfast. However, he dared not leave until he found out how Lieutenant Harnett was faring.

His legs aching from his many trips up and down the ladder that day, Tib cautiously pushed open the trapdoor. The loft was almost dark, but the small amount of twilight coming in through the single window enabled him to make out the still form of the lieutenant.

Tib could not see the man's face, but his breathing seemed more normal. And when Tib touched Harnett's forehead, he found it wet with sweat.

The fever had broken!

Lieutenant Harnett would be all right—that is, if the British didn't catch him!

The hunger Tib felt had increased, once his anxiety over the lieutenant had eased. Quickly he piled hay over the sleeping man so the night air would not chill the sweat-drenched soldier. Then he slowly climbed down the ladder and walked back to the farmhouse.

9

Anxious Waiting

LITTLE REMAINED OF THE MUTTON LEG, which his uncle had left uncovered on the kitchen table. His guest gone, Uncle Edward had settled down in front of the large kitchen fire, a tankard in his hand, for the coming of night had brought a chill wind, not unusual for the Hudson Valley even in July.

Tib had just finished his supper of bread, tea, and cold mutton, when his uncle stood and yawned. "I'm off to bed, Tib," he said. "Check the horses before you retire. Call me if anything is amiss."

Without another word, Uncle Edward went off toward the only bedroom in the farmhouse. Tib's own small bed was in a corner of the kitchen, but he would not sleep there tonight, he knew.

"If the horse is restless, I may sleep in the barn," Tib called out to the retreating back of his uncle.

The older man turned slightly, saying over his shoulder,

"Your intense interest surprises me, Tib. But do as you will. However, you would do well to remember that a night spent in the barn will not excuse you from your duties on the morrow." Then he was gone.

With a sigh of relief, Tib sat by the fire, listening for the sounds of snoring that would signal Uncle Edward's slumber. However, the moon had already risen and Tib was dozing in his chair when finally the heavy sounds came from behind the closed door of the bedroom.

Tib hastily stirred up the fire, placing the pieces of mutton he had saved into a pot of water, along with a pinch of dried rosemary and a little salt. It wouldn't make much of a broth, but it would give the sick man some strength when he woke up. At least Tib hoped the lieutenant would wake up with a clear mind.

But what if he didn't? What if he was still delirious and thought Tib to be a deserter again? A tremor of fear shot through him when Tib recalled the musket pointed at him.

For that reason, Tib's steps were cautious as he ascended the ladder, the pot of steaming broth in one hand, lantern in the other. Pushing up the trapdoor with his head and shoulders, he quickly stepped onto the floor of the loft, lantern raised high.

Where was Lieutenant Harnett?

A loud BANG echoed through the loft.

Tib spun around as if the lieutenant's musket had found its mark.

But it hadn't, and Tib began to laugh nervously.

"Just closing the shutter," came the lieutenant's clear voice. "We mustn't let the light show from the window, Tib."

The boy stood staring until at last he could speak. "You're standing!" he finally managed to gasp.

"Just barely," Jason Harnett confessed, as he slid down to a sitting position. "What happened, Tib? When last I remember it was afternoon."

While the lieutenant sipped the broth, Tib recounted all that had happened. He had just gotten to the part about waiting for Uncle Edward to fall asleep, when cracking sounds erupted in the distance.

Harnett's blue eyes were immediately alert. He listened for a few minutes, then asked, "What day is it, Tib? It seems I've lost count."

"Why, it's July fifteenth."

The cracking sounds were coming faster now.

"Then they've done it! They've made it over the mountains after all!"

Seeing Tib's bewildered face, the lieutenant explained, "It's Wayne's Light Infantry, Tib. They're attacking the British at Stony Point!"

"Hurrah!" Tib shouted, then clamped his hand over his

mouth when he realized the noise he had made.

The lieutenant grinned widely at the boy's reaction. "And now I must be going," he told Tib, as he struggled to his feet. "As weak as I am, I'd be no use at the fort. But I can do some good back at West Point."

"I'll help you," Tib offered immediately.

"Oh, no, lad!" Harnett protested. "You've done enough already. And the noise of the battle will soon awaken your uncle. If he finds you are gone . . ."

Tib shook his head stubbornly, then pointed to the swaying, trembling man before him. "You'd never make it. The British would capture you within the hour—that is, if you didn't fall over some cliff first. Now, let us go."

"Tib, it's too dangerous. . ."

Tib continued to shake his head, as he started toward the ladder.

The lieutenant stumbled after him, his voice noticeably weaker from the strain of arguing. "And if we do get to West Point—what then, Tib? What will you do?"

"Go south to Morristown," the boy answered briefly. He was already part way down the ladder, his hand extended to help the lieutenant.

"But Tib . . ."

"I was leaving anyway," Tib interrupted, "for I can stay here no longer."

Defeated, the lieutenant followed Tib down the ladder. He had little faith in his ability to travel the difficult route back to West Point. Though it was less than ten miles to the north, those miles were made much longer by the mountainous terrain. But so long as there was breath still in his body, the brave lieutenant knew he must try.

He looked over at Tib with a smile. After all, if a mere boy had the courage to try for Morristown—more than forty miles away—certainly an officer of the North Carolina Brigade could attempt the perilous journey to West Point.

10

Perilous Journey

As soon as they were past the cleared fields of Uncle Edward's farm, Tib began to doubt that Jason Harnett would ever make it to West Point. But every time Tib looked at him worriedly, the lieutenant would grin, his face ghostly in the pale moonlight.

"We seem to be heading east instead of north," Harnett panted, when they stopped for a moment.

Tib nodded. "We've got to skirt around the Dunderberg, and it's easier to begin this far south of it," he explained.

"The Dunderberg?" Harnett repeated, then nodded. "Oh, yes, the mountain. When General Wayne landed on Sandy Beach north of here, his plan was to go all the way around the Dunderberg from the west."

"Then he's attacking from land, not from the Hudson side of Stony Point."

Jason Harnett sighed. "Aye, Tib—the most dangerous side,

where the British have planted sharpened stakes that can skewer a man like a roasting pig. I've heard tell that General Wayne's fellow officers called it madness when Wayne presented his plan to General Washington. But if anyone can do it, Wayne can."

"I hope so," Tib murmured, then added, "We'd better start again."

"Tib?"

The boy turned, thinking the lieutenant needed help to get up, but Harnett was already standing, his eyes straining into the darkness.

"Tib, since we're going east anyway, do you think ... I mean, is there a spot of land overlooking ..."

"Stony Point?" Tib finished the question for him. "The danger will be great," Tib said slowly. "But just north of the point, there's ..."

The lieutenant's voice was low but intense. "Let us take the chance, Tib," he said. "I must see if Wayne's attack is successful. If I never make it to West Point, then at least I will know. I *must* know, Tib!"

Tib's own voice was shaking when he answered, "All right, we'll go." Then he went on, "And you'll make it to West Point, too. I'll see that you do!"

But Tib was far from confident as he led the lieutenant through the dense woods. The detour would take them at least a mile out of their way, and the lieutenant was growing weaker with every step.

Since he was in front, Tib saw the moonlight-sparkled waters of the Hudson River before Lieutenant Harnett did. But Tib did not say anything until they had climbed a small knoll.

"There, to your right," Tib directed. "That's Stony Point."

As both of them stared at the dark knob of land which jutted out into the Hudson, they realized they could hear no gunfire. Surely, if the Americans were storming the point, there would be some sound. But the summer's night was strangely —frighteningly—silent.

Jason Harnett leaned against a tree. "The British must have stopped them at the abatis."

"The what?" Tib asked.

"The abatis. Sharpened stakes set in mounds of earth to repel the enemy," Harnett explained slowly. "If Wayne got past the abatis, surely we would be able to see something from here, or at least hear the sounds of battle. No, Tib, I'm afraid it was all in vain and that the British still hold Stony Point."

Harnett had slumped to a sitting position, his voice showing his discouragement as he went on, "We needed a victory so badly. If only—"

His words were suddenly cut off by Tib's hand across his lips, and he fell back under the boy's pushing weight. The two landed in a patch of mountain laurel, whose woody branches gouged into them cruelly.

The startled lieutenant struggled only a minute, Tib's hand still over his mouth, until he, too, heard the horses approaching.

"Who goes there?" demanded a deep voice. "Who goes there, I say?"

"Have an ounce of sense, Harry!" came another voice. "That sound was probably made by some wild creature in the brush. But you might have been challenging a bevy of rebels. Who knows how many Wayne brought with him."

There was a muttered oath, then the first voice replied, "You're right, of course. Losers don't attack. They fall back to fight another day. Come, let's get out of here!"

The horses' hoofs thudded dully on the soft earth as the two riders sped away, but not before Tib had spied the brilliant scarlet of a British uniform.

"Did you hear what he said?" Tib turned to Lieutenant Harnett. "He said 'losers.' That means Wayne took Stony Point!"

Using Long John as a crutch, Harnett struggled to his feet, then shouldered the long musket as he stumbled to the edge of the trees. Taking a spyglass from one of the deep pockets of his coat, he trained it on a spot of light now visible on the crest of Stony Point.

For long moments he studied the spot, then handed the

spyglass to Tib. "There, lad, look where they have lighted a bonfire. Then draw the glass upward to a spot above the trees."

Tib saw it immediately and his heart raced in wild excitement as the flickering firelight illuminated the banner now flying from the flagpole.

"It's ours!" he shouted. "That's our flag!" Then remembering where he was, he added in a triumphant whisper, "Wayne has taken Stony Point!"

"Indeed, it would seem so," Harnett replied proudly.

"Why don't we go there?" Tib asked. "It's closer than West Point."

The lieutenant's head was shaking from side to side even before Tib finished his sentence. "The fighting may still be going on, and we have no way of knowing if Wayne will be able to hold his position. Plus that, the woods between are probably full of Redcoats. No, Tib, it must be West Point."

As he stood up, Tib could feel his weary muscles complain. If he was this tired, how must Jason Harnett feel? How would they ever make it to West Point?

As if he had read Tib's thoughts, the lieutenant said softly, "In the event I don't make it, Tib, you must bring the word to West Point."

"We'll both bring the word!" Tib said stoutly, then struck out toward the north, with Jason Harnett trying his best to keep up.

11

A Daring Ruse

THEY TRUDGED ON, hour after weary hour, bumping into rocks and trees, stumbling over the stone fences that marked some farmer's attempt to till the mountainous area. Always Tib was there, urging the weakened lieutenant on, helping him up when he fell, giving a supporting arm as they crossed streams and other barriers that soon exhausted what little strength the lieutenant had.

Finally, Jason Harnett gasped, "I must rest for a moment, Tib. My legs are numb. I can go no farther."

The boy bent over him. But the lieutenant could not hear Tib's anxious questions. For Jason Harnett had become unconscious the minute his body touched the ground.

When the lieutenant did not stir after a few minutes, Tib's worry flared into fright, and he searched the area nearby, hoping to find a stream. He came across one soon enough, almost stumbling into it as it foamed across its pebbled bed, bringing its mountain-chilled water to the Hudson far to Tib's right.

Wishing he had a canteen, Tib soaked his handkerchief in the stream, returning to bathe the lieutenant's face as best he could. But there was no response from the unconscious man, and Tib made his way back to the stream for more water.

He was just dipping his handkerchief into the stream for the second time, when he heard the sound of snapping twigs. Someone was moving through the bushes.

The British?

Tib ducked back into the underbrush which bordered the stream, his eyes searching the moon-dappled darkness.

There was a faint gleam as the moonlight was reflected on a bayonet, then a horse and rider emerged from the woods on the other side of the stream. Quickly dismounting, the rider led his horse to the water. "Now, drink your fill," Tib heard him say. "Then I'll work on that rock you've got wedged in your shoe."

It was a soldier—the bayonet-pointed musket quickly told Tib that—but he was not British!

Tib was just about to emerge from his hiding place, when something told him to stop. Even if the soldier were not British, would he believe him? Would he help him bring Lieutenant Harnett to West Point? What if the soldier were a deserter or a British spy?

A plan was forming in his mind, even before Tib was aware that he was silently slipping back through the woods to where Jason Harnett lay unconscious. All Tib knew was that if the lieutenant didn't get help soon, he might die. And lying on the dew-chilled ground as he was would certainly hasten his death.

Pausing only a moment to place the wet handkerchief on the lieutenant's now feverish forehead, Tib picked up Long John and stealthily made his way back to the stream.

Yes, the soldier was still on the bank of the narrow stream. As he bent over one of the horse's hoofs, his back was to Tib, while his bayonet-tipped musket was on the ground beside him. "There now, the stone's out," he spoke to the horse.

The man began to straighten up just as Tib's voice rang out, "Stand fast!"

The soldier jerked erect, then made a move for his gun.

"Hold or I'll shoot!" Tib declared menacingly.

The man halted immediately, raising his arms in a gesture of surrender.

"A boy!" the soldier exclaimed, when Tib had splashed across the stream to stand in front of him.

"A boy with a musket!" Tib corrected. "Now lead your horse across the stream."

"What is it you want from me?" the soldier asked fearfully.

"I have no cause to harm you," Tib assured him, his own heart thudding painfully. "I just need your horse for a few hours."

Picking up the soldier's musket, Tib directed the man and horse across the stream, then into the woods where Jason Harnett still lay unconscious.

"Pick him up and put him across the saddle," Tib ordered. "Secure him well so he doesn't fall off."

The soldier bent over the still form, then spun around quickly—but not as quickly as Tib raised the muzzle of Long John.

"Go on with your work," Tib told him harshly, glad that the moonlight was not strong enough to reveal his trembling hands.

The soldier placed the unconscious lieutenant across the saddle, then turned to face Tib. "Who are you?" he demanded. "This is an American soldier. Where are you taking him?"

"Secure him," Tib ordered. "Then we'll be on our way to West Point."

"West Point!" the soldier exclaimed. "Why, that's exactly . . ."

"Enough talk!" Tib interrupted. "The road will be dangerous, and we'd best use our ears instead of our lips."

"But—"

"Enough, I said!" and Tib pushed the muzzle of Long

John against the soldier's stomach.

All that could be heard was the soft thump of hoofs and the muffled jingle of the horse's bridle as they made their way north toward West Point.

12

Reward for Bravery

EXHAUSTION HAD OVERTAKEN Tib shortly after they arrived at West Point, and he had slept, sitting straight up, in the chair next to Lieutenant Harnett's bed. But weariness had not prevented the nightmares from intruding in his sleep—nightmares of what would happen to him for waylaying the soldier near the stream.

So it was that Tib anxiously sat by Harnett's bedside, remembering the anger of the captain to whom he had been brought when they reached West Point early this morning.

The captain's anger had cooled somewhat, though, when he had recognized Jason Harnett. Therefore, when Tib had insisted on staying by the lieutenant's bedside, the captain had nodded his permission, while ominously saying they would "settle matters" when Jason Harnett woke up.

It seemed to Tib that the lieutenant was about to do just that, for his eyelids had fluttered slightly and his fever-weakened body stirred restlessly.

Rising from his chair, Tib went to the door, softly calling to the orderly outside, "Tell the captain he's waking up now."

Seconds later, the lieutenant opened his eyes to see the face of his superior officer. "Captain Lewis!" he whispered in disbelief. "But you're . . . you're in . . ."

"In West Point," the captain nodded. "And so are you, Jason, though I'm not sure I approve of the way you got here."

His blue eyes confused, Jason Harnett was about to ask the captain what he meant when the officer called, "Come here, lad."

Tib was soon standing beside Captain Lewis. The boy's face was pale from worry.

"It seems that when you lost consciousness in the woods south of here, this young fellow waylaid one of our own messengers who was on his way here."

Tib gasped in surprise. So that was what the soldier had been trying to tell him.

The captain's voice was stern as he went on, "The lad stopped our messenger by threatening him with a musket— your own musket, I might add!"

Tib felt Lieutenant Harnett's eyes upon him, but he did not look up. "Tib," the lieutenant spoke gently, "didn't you know that Long John was empty?"

Tib was sure his face was red because his cheeks were as

hot as if he had a sunburn. "I knew," he answered, "but I had to get you here."

A sound somewhere between a snort and a cough erupted from Captain Lewis, forcing Tib to look up. The stern frown had left the captain's face and his lips were twitching as if he were trying to suppress a smile. Finally giving up, the officer let out a full-throated chuckle.

"And get you here he did, Jason," the captain went on. "He forced the messenger to bring you here on his horse. Only then did the messenger find out the musket was empty! Now I don't know whether we must arrest the lad or reward him."

"Reward him, for you don't know half of what Tib's done for me," Harnett answered quickly. Then he turned his eyes back to Tib. "Did you tell him what we saw at Stony Point?"

"He gave me no chance," Tib answered truthfully, and again the captain gave his odd little snort-cough.

Harnett looked back at the captain. "We saw the flag—our flag—flying over the British garrison," Harnett related triumphantly. Then his still-weak voice became lower. "However, I have no way of knowing if Wayne was able to hold his position."

"Tib should have asked the messenger he waylaid," Captain Lewis told them. "The messenger was bringing word from Stony Point that Wayne's position was secure—that Stony

Point is indeed ours!"

Tib felt like shouting, "Hurrah!" But he didn't want to take any chance of angering the captain again, so he remained silent. There was a happy smile on his face though, and it became broader when Jason Harnett reached out to clasp his hand.

As he did so, the jubilant captain rushed on, "Who would have thought Wayne could do it with barely thirteen hundred men armed only with muskets. It was a daring attack, to be sure. In fact, he's earned himself the name of 'Mad' Anthony Wayne. Let me tell you, Jason—"

The captain stopped abruptly, for Jason Harnett's eyes were studying Tib. "Brave Tib," Harnett said softly. "You had your own part in the storming of Stony Point, didn't you?"

"How so?" Captain Lewis demanded.

"The story's a long one, so for now I'll just say that Tib kept me hidden—on a Tory farm, no less! Tib's loyalty deserves reward."

The captain eyed Tib for a few silent moments, then he asked Harnett, "What would you recommend?"

Tib's eyes brightened with hope. Would Harnett remember?

"Tib wants to go to Morristown."

"Impossible!" the captain exclaimed. "Why, Morristown is fifty miles away or more. The roads are swarming with Red-coats who'll be especially watchful now that we took Stony Point away from them. Not only that, but . . ."

"There's always the Corduroy Road," Harnett pointed out, unmindful that he was interrupting his superior officer.

"Jason!" Captain Lewis exploded. "You know that is a secret military road used only for vital communications and supplies!"

Before he answered, the lieutenant reached over to grip Tib's shoulder, as if to reassure him that everything would be all right. Then he turned back to Captain Lewis. "Don't we have to send the news of Stony Point to Morristown? Why not enlist Tib as a temporary dispatch-carrier, with his service to end once he gets to Morristown?"

"We've already sent word to Morristown!" the captain protested.

"Why not send another message?" Harnett persisted. "To make sure the word gets through?"

Captain Lewis seemed to hold his breath for a minute, his face getting redder and redder. Tib was afraid that his friend had gone too far—that Captain Lewis might throw them both in the guardhouse. But then the captain let out another one of his snort-coughs, followed by an exasperated sigh. Sitting down on the edge of Harnett's bed, he began to chuckle.

"And with a full pardon for stopping a messenger of the Continental Army at musket point, I suppose?"

"Of course," Jason Harnett agreed, then began chuckling too, his arm around the now smiling boy.

13

The Corduroy Road

ACTUALLY, there was a message Captain Lewis wanted to send to Morristown, as Tib discovered the next morning when he went to say good-bye to Jason Harnett.

"It's as good news as the success at Stony Point," Captain Lewis told Tib, as they stood next to the lieutenant's bed in the West Point Infirmary. "And it's important that the message reaches Morristown as soon as possible."

"Yes, sir," Tib said in what he hoped was a military voice.

"You see," Captain Lewis went on, "General Wayne was wounded during the battle . . ."

"Oh, no!" cried the lieutenant, and his words were echoed by Tib.

"Such discouraging news is bad for the men of our army. Goodness knows they have enough to discourage them, what with the lack of supplies and Clinton's brutal raid on Connecticut. Anyway, Tib, you are to bring word that while General Wayne was wounded during the storming of Stony Point, he was not badly hurt. He'll be back leading his men before the week is out."

"Hurrah!" shouted Tib.

The captain's face grew stern, and Tib thought he was angry at his outburst. But this was not so, as he soon found out.

"The way to Morristown is long and fraught with danger," Captain Lewis told him. "And I'm still not certain it is wise to send you. But Lieutenant Harnett knows you better than I do, and he says you are truly a man in a boy's body."

Tib felt his face flush with pride, and he wanted to thank Jason Harnett. However, the captain was still speaking.

"I have arranged for you to be escorted to the beginning of the Corduroy Road, which is about fifteen miles from here. From there you are on your own. To the south, our secret highway connects with other roads that will take you to Morristown."

"There should be enough soldiers along the way for you to ask directions, if need be," Lieutenant Harnett spoke up. "Just show them your pass."

Captain Lewis nodded. "And remember, Tib, tell everyone you see of the victory at Stony Point, and that General Wayne is alive and well."

"I will do my best," Tib told him solemnly.

"I'm sure you will," Captain Lewis said. "Now, I'll be off to see about your pass, Tib, while you and Jason say farewell."

The lieutenant's blue eyes were sympathetic as Tib struggled to find words more adequate than just "good-bye."

"It's because of you, Tib, that I'm even here to say farewell," Harnett began. "And I shall always be grateful to you."

Gripping the boy's hand, he went on, "Tell me what you'll do once you get to Morristown. You said you have an aunt there?"

"Yes, her name is Jenny Bucks and she lives just south of Morristown on the Jockey Hollow Road."

"Jenny Bucks . . . Jockey Hollow Road," the lieutenant repeated. "I'll remember that, Tib. For perhaps we'll meet again there."

"Do you really think we might?"

"Washington camped there during the winter of '77," Harnett answered. "Perhaps he may again. If he does and Wayne's brigade is with him, we shall meet again."

"I hope we do," Tib said earnestly.

"I hope so too. Now, you'd best be on your way. The sun is already high and it's many miles to Morristown."

At the door of the infirmary, Tib turned to look back at his friend. The lieutenant was sitting up on the cot, his hand raised in a silent salute to the boy he had known for such a short but unforgettable time.

It was a good thing Tib had no idea of what the Corduroy Road would be like. For had he expected to see a regular thoroughfare, he would have been sadly disappointed.

When the soldier Captain Lewis had sent along pointed down the narrow avenue, Tib's eyes opened wide in amazement.

Stretching before him through the woods was an uneven primitive trail, hardly wider than a farm wagon. The roadbed itself was made up of rough-hewn logs laid side by side, crosswise, with the tips forming the outer edges of the road.

"Is that the Corduroy Road?" he asked the soldier.

"That she be," the man answered. "Rough and ready, and not very comfortable to ride on, but her thick logs make a firm foundation for the heavy ammunition wagons. So she's done her part in keeping the lines open between Morristown and West Point."

Reining his horse around, the soldier told him, "Just follow her straight. That nag you've got will do you if you don't push him too hard. If anybody questions you, just show your pass. Now, good-bye—and good luck, boy."

Tib watched the soldier gallop away, then urged his own horse down the narrow road. The trees grew thickly, seeming to push against the sides of the road as if they wished to cover over the narrow swath man had cut through their midst. Above, their gently swaying tops almost met, leaving only a small band of blue sky.

Waiting for his eyes to adjust to the sun-dappled gloom of the forest, Tib shivered. Try as he might, he could not recall even one detail of the map Captain Lewis had shown him back at West Point. No copy had been given to Tib—the vital road was too well guarded a secret. Tib must memorize what he saw or do without.

Oh, what were some of the names he had seen on the map?

Tib felt panic grip his heart. Then, suddenly, he remembered something his father used to say: "The best cure for fear is air." Tib wasn't so sure that it would work now, but he began taking slow, deep breaths, counting up to seven each time he exhaled or inhaled.

Whether it was the deep breaths or the thought of his father, Tib did not know, but names began popping into his head: the Sterling Iron Works, where his father had, in 1778, helped forge the chain that spanned the Hudson River to prevent a British attack on West Point. Yes, Sterling had been drawn on the map, but not the small iron furnace where his father had been working at the time of his death.

Blinking back the tears that always formed when he thought of that dreadful day three months ago, Tib forced himself to concentrate on the map he had seen.

Bear Hill was to the north, while to the southwest would be the iron mines at Ringwood, where Robert Erskine had been manager before he became General Washington's mapmaker. In fact, it had been Erskine himself who had laid out the Corduroy Road.

But remembering these names made Tib recall other, less

pleasant things too, and he glanced fearfully around at the trees so close on either side.

He had heard many a story of marauding Indians, and now there was the added threat of those Indians who were being paid by the British to harass the Americans.

And here within the Ramapo Mountains, there was even greater danger from the outlaws that plundered the countryside murdering anyone who got in their way. They called themselves Tories, but their only loyalty was to themselves. It was true that the infamous Claudius Smith, called the Scourge of the Ramapos, had been captured earlier this year and had been hanged at Goshen. But part of his gang, and other outlaws too, still roamed these mountains.

When his horse snorted, ears pricked forward, Tib almost fell out of the saddle. The horse had sensed something. But what?

Tib's eyes darted from tree to tree. There. Over there. Was that something moving behind that shagbark oak?

A man stepped out from behind the tree, his brown jacket blending in with the background almost as if he was one of the forest creatures.

"What ho, lad!" he called cheerily.

Remembering that he was to spread the word about the victory at Stony Point, Tib almost reined in his horse. But before he had pulled back on the leather strips between his fingers,

Tib's heels dug into the startled horse's flanks.

The animal snorted his protest, but being an Army horse, he obeyed immediately and leaped forward, his hoofs thudding on the wooden logs.

Expecting that any minute a musket ball might rip through his back, Tib bent low over the saddle, urging the horse on as fast as possible over the log road.

What had made him take flight? he wondered. Then Tib thought of the man's jacket. It had been of a fine brown material, not the homespun of the farmer or the leather of the hunter. What could a man like that be doing out here in the middle of the woods? Tib did not know—and he didn't relish the thought of staying around to find out!

As the horse rounded a curve in the Corduroy Road, Tib chanced a look behind him. The man still stood there, but he had been joined by five or six others who must have been hiding in the woods. All of them held muskets!

Were they outlaws? Tib had no time to think about it as he saw ahead of him the shimmering blue water of a lake. After making sure he was not being followed, Tib pulled back on the reins, slowing the horse to a walk. If there was danger behind him, there was danger ahead as well. For Captain Lewis had warned him about the treacherous stretches near the lakes and rivers.

"Take care that you don't step off the Corduroy Road, lad,"

he had said. "For the rains were heavy this spring and the mud is still as deep as a wagon axle. The logs on the Corduroy Road are also apt to slip or shift, so mind you to walk your horse, else he might break a leg."

Whether it was Tuxedo Lake, or Bear Lake, or Cannonball Lake farther to the south, Tib could not be sure, for he was too busy concentrating on the rough logs immediately before him.

Suddenly the horse lurched to the left, his foreleg slipping between two of the logs. Had he not been alert, Tib would have landed on his head, but he hung on to the horse's mane until the animal recovered itself. Then they proceeded slowly around the western edge of the lake and were soon on firm ground again.

On they went—sometimes slowly, sometimes at a trot—until Tib could feel his bones aching from the jolting gait of the horse. Now he was thankful for the wall of trees on either side of him, for they sheltered him from the hot July sun that occasionally sent burning rays down through a break in the leafy canopy overhead.

Tib was wondering where he should stop to rest the horse when he heard muffled shouts up ahead. Fear made his empty stomach tighten, and his mouth grew dry as he stopped to listen.

The shouts continued—not cries for help, but the kind of

shouts men make when hard at work. So Tib urged the horse forward.

They had reached the crest of a hill when Tib spied the cause of the shouting. Halfway up the other side, a large wagon was being unloaded by four men, all of them dressed in ragged homespun uniforms.

With a joyful cry of greeting, Tib approached them. For the first time since he started his journey he was aware of how lonely he had been in the silence of the forest.

However, he was greeted by scowls—except for one man, who seemed to be in charge of the group. Though this man did not scowl, his expression was disbelieving when Tib explained he was on his way to Morristown to deliver a message from West Point.

Before the man could speak, though, a red-headed soldier grumbled, "Well, if this isn't a day to end all days! First we can't get this wagonload of cannonballs up the hill, and now here comes a mere boy saying he's a messenger from West Point!" As he spoke, the red-headed man sat down on the ground, quickly followed by the other two.

"Get that wagon unloaded," the leader ordered irritably. "A little less complaining and a little more work are what we need to get us to the top of the hill."

"Aw, Sergeant, it's so hot, and the horses are as tired as we are. Give us a few minutes."

The sergeant hesitated a moment, then nodded to the man as he gestured for Tib to dismount. "It's past noon anyway," he said. "We've only cold rations, lad, but perhaps you will join us while you tell us how it is that you are traveling this road."

Tib could sense that the sergeant didn't believe him, so he dug into his boot top and produced the pass Captain Lewis had given him.

"Well, I'll be!" the sergeant exclaimed. "It's true enough. Why would they choose a mere lad like you?"

Without going into detail about his own adventures on that night, Tib told the men about General Wayne's successful storming of Stony Point.

"Aye, we heard about that," nodded the sergeant.

Then the red-headed man who had been complaining spoke up. "But where's the success," he asked, "when we lost one of our best generals?"

"If you mean General Wayne, you're wrong!" Tib declared. "It's true that Wayne was injured, but it was only a slight wound."

"How would you know?" the man challenged.

"Because that is the message I'm bringing to Morristown—that Wayne will be back at the head of his troops next week at the latest."

The jubilant shout from the men startled the horses and

echoed against the rocks of the hillside. Even the sergeant could not restrain a happy "Hurrah!"

Tib held out his hand to the grinning sergeant. "I thank you for sharing your meal with me, but now I must be going."

"And so must we!" said the red-headed soldier, who had done the grumbling. Scrambling to his feet, he cried to the others, "Come on, you lazy laggards. Unload that wagon so it's light enough for the horses to pull up the hill! We must get these cannonballs north to West Point!"

Amazed at the sudden change in the man, Tib turned to the sergeant. The older man clasped Tib's hand and said, "My thanks to you, Tib, for bringing the good word. Garvey over there," and he pointed to the red-headed man, "is a good soldier. He was just discouraged—in fact, we all were."

Tib nodded as he looked over at the men who were now hard at work. Then, after warning the sergeant of the outlaws he had met earlier in the day, Tib mounted his horse and headed south along the Corduroy Road.

14

On to Morristown

THE SUN WAS NOW a burning white ball in the sky, and Tib could feel the energy being drained from his body. It would have been nice to stretch out on the bank of one of the many streams he passed, but Morristown was still a good distance away, and he hoped to get there before dark.

He had traveled only a short distance when the log bed of the Corduroy Road ended abruptly. Up ahead was a crossroads. But there were no roadsigns, not even a stone mile marker to tell Tib which way to go.

Reining in his horse, Tib tried to remember the map Captain Lewis had shown him. Why hadn't he looked more closely?

Panic once more quickened his breathing, and Tib forced himself to take slow, deep breaths, just as his father had taught him to do.

Within minutes he felt better, though he still had no idea

which road to take. He knew Morristown was somewhere to the southwest. But knowing this was not help enough, for two of the roads in front of him appeared to run south.

There was only one thing to do: Wait until someone came along who could tell him which road to take.

Leading his horse into the trees bordering the crossroads, Tib took up a position where he could see anybody approaching, without that person seeing him.

But what if no one came?

Angry for allowing the question to pop into his mind, Tib concentrated on trying to remember the map Captain Lewis had shown him. No matter how hard he tried, though, the same question forced its way back into his mind: What if no one came?

"Then I'll take the road which seems the most likely choice," he said out loud, hoping that would settle the matter. It did in a way, but then another question arose: Which road was the most likely choice?

"I'll decide on that later," Tib told himself, and stretched out on the ground between two trees.

It was because of this that Tib sensed the soldiers' approach before he could see or hear them. The vibrations in the earth beneath him warned him that someone was coming, and he leaped to his feet, straining his eyes to see down the three roads that led from the clearing.

A combination of fear and hope made his breath come faster. But this time Tib was too busy trying to see who was coming to take his father's advice.

So it was that Tib could barely muster a breathless shout when he saw the rag-tag uniforms of the sullen-faced soldiers who marched in front of a small convoy of supply wagons.

"Who goes there?" came a challenging cry, as the lead soldier raised his musket.

"A messenger from West Point!" Tib managed to answer, as he fearfully eyed the musket. "As you can see, I'm not armed."

"Advance, lad," the soldier answered, but he did not lower his musket.

Tib came forward slowly, his pass from Captain Lewis held in his outstretched hand. Once he had read it, the soldier seemed to relax his hold on the musket.

"I know the war is going badly," he said, "but you're the youngest Army messenger I've ever seen."

"It's not as bad as you might think," Tib told him. Then he related the news of Stony Point and General Wayne's injury.

A broad smile came across the soldier's haggard face. Before answering Tib, he called behind him, "Gather round, men, and hear this lad's news!"

Once Tib had told the men, excited shouts and questions

crackled through the hot afternoon air. Finally, the voices subsided and the men lounged around, some leaning on the supply wagons, while others gathered in small groups talking quietly.

It was then the lead soldier motioned for Tib to follow him a few yards away from the group.

"You've done me a great service, lad," he said softly. "Now tell me how I can repay you."

The seriousness of the soldier's voice brought a puzzled frown to Tib's forehead. "I'd appreciate your telling me the right road to Morristown," he answered. "But as for the great service you speak of, I only . . ."

"You may have prevented a mutiny," the soldier told him. "For many miles I have suspected a plot was afoot. The men are tired of this war. They worry about their families back home, especially since they haven't been paid for almost three months. General Washington has promised they will be paid soon, but promises can't be worn on their feet or be cooked for dinner."

The soldier paused to look back at his men, and smiled when he heard someone begin to whistle a marching tune. "They are patriots, each and every one of them, but hunger and illness and . . . and . . ."

"And discouragement," Tib supplied the word.

"Yes, discouragement—it's worse than a musket ball. That's

why I say you have done me a great service, Tib. But you have done an even greater service to these men, for I feel your news has swayed them from committing a rash act they would have regretted the rest of their lives."

Together, they watched the men around the wagons. Their uniforms were still ragged, but their faces were no longer sullen. Smiling again, the soldier said, "Now it's the road to Morristown you want, correct?" When Tib nodded, he went on, "Take the fork to the right, and you should be in Morristown before sundown. If in doubt, though, you'll find plenty of soldiers on the road south of here."

As the soldier spoke, Tib glanced back at the narrow roadway made up of logs laid side by side, like the ribs in a piece of corduroy cloth. Noticing his look, the soldier asked, "You came down by the Corduroy Road, huh?"

"Yes," Tib replied, his eyes still on the secret highway.

"She's not a very pretty bit of engineering," the soldier went on, "but she's served us well."

As Tib rode away, he thought about what the soldier had said. Yes, the Corduroy Road had served him well, too—first as a dream, a hope—and now as a reality.

Someday he might be traveling back up this very same road to fulfill another dream—the dream of an independent country. For Tib had decided, should the war still be in progress, when he was old enough he was going to join the Continental Army. Jason Harnett had told him he would be a good soldier, and that was exactly what he was going to be!

So with this new dream to guide him, Tiberius Wade, Jr.—special messenger for the Continental Army—rode on to Morristown.

The Author

PATRICIA EDWARDS CLYNE was born in New York City and graduated with a BA degree in journalism from Hunter College. She has worked as a reporter and also as a free-lance editor.

Early childhood visit to Ozark Mountain caves resulted in a lifelong interest which is now centered on rock shelters of the Northeast, many of which she has investigated and photographed for her articles and stories.

Her love of history and exploring also has taken her to numerous locations connected with the American Revolution, including the area around Stony Point, the setting for *The Corduroy Road*. Her desire to pass on the history and sense of pride and patriotism Americans felt has led to this story for young people.

Mrs. Clyne lives in New York with her husband and four sons, who all share her love of exploring and hiking. This is her first book for children.

The Illustrator

CARY STUDIED AT the Massachusetts College of Art before launching his career as an advertising artist. After ten years in the commercial field, he moved to his present home in West Barnstable, Massachusetts, where he paints, does free-lance illustrating, acts in productions of the local drama club, and goes fishing. Cary and his wife have three children "and all the usual excitements that go along with these."